MAKE IT MONSTER

The Great Sandcastle Competition

Written by James Clements
Illustrated by Richard Watson

OXFORD
UNIVERSITY PRESS

It was the day of The Great Sandcastle Competition. Ralf, Scooter, Netty, and Cora were very excited.

'I have got some buckets and spades!' said Cora, excitedly.

I have got some buckets too!

Cora Ralf Netty Scooter

How many buckets has Cora got? Three is a **part**. How many buckets has Ralf got? Two is a **part**. How many buckets do they have **altogether**? The **whole** is five.

'Have you got any buckets or spades, Scooter?' asked Netty.

'I've got something better than buckets and spades,' he replied.

'I've made a sandcastle-making machine!' said Scooter. 'I haven't had time to test it yet, but I am sure it will work perfectly.'

On the beach, the judges told everyone about the competition.

'There will be two prizes,' said one judge. 'One prize will be for the team that makes the most sandcastle towers.'

'The other prize will be for the sandcastle with the best decorations,' said the second judge. 'You can use anything to decorate your sandcastle. Last year, the winners used shells and flags.'

How many flags are on each tower? How many flags are there **altogether**? What are the **parts**? What is the **whole**? The **parts** are three, three, and three. The **whole** is nine.

The friends found a space on the beach next to some other monsters.

Ralf, Netty, and Cora started to make short towers with their buckets. Scooter started to make tall towers with his machine.

After a while, the friends stopped to count how many towers they had **altogether**.

'There are more tall towers than short ones!' said Scooter.

How many short towers are there? How many tall towers are there? How many towers are there **altogether**? What are the **parts**? What is the **whole**? The **parts** are two and four. The **whole** is six.

'Well done!' said one of the other monsters, with a big smile. 'You've built lots of towers.'

'Thank you!' said Ralf, smiling back.

Ralf looked across to see how many towers the other monsters had built.

'They have built lots of towers, too!' he whispered to his friends.

'How many can you see?' asked Netty.

Find two types of towers in the picture. How many towers of each type are there? What are the **parts**? What is the **whole**? The **parts** are three and five. The **whole** is eight.

‘They have eight towers **altogether**,’ said Ralf.

‘That’s more towers than we have!’ exclaimed Netty.

‘Don’t worry, we can still win,’ said Scooter. He pressed a large red button.

The machine went faster and faster. Sand flew everywhere.

Then there was a loud noise and cogs and springs began to fly out of the machine!

With one last loud crunch, the machine shuddered and finally stopped.

Ralf and Cora collected the cogs and springs in their buckets.

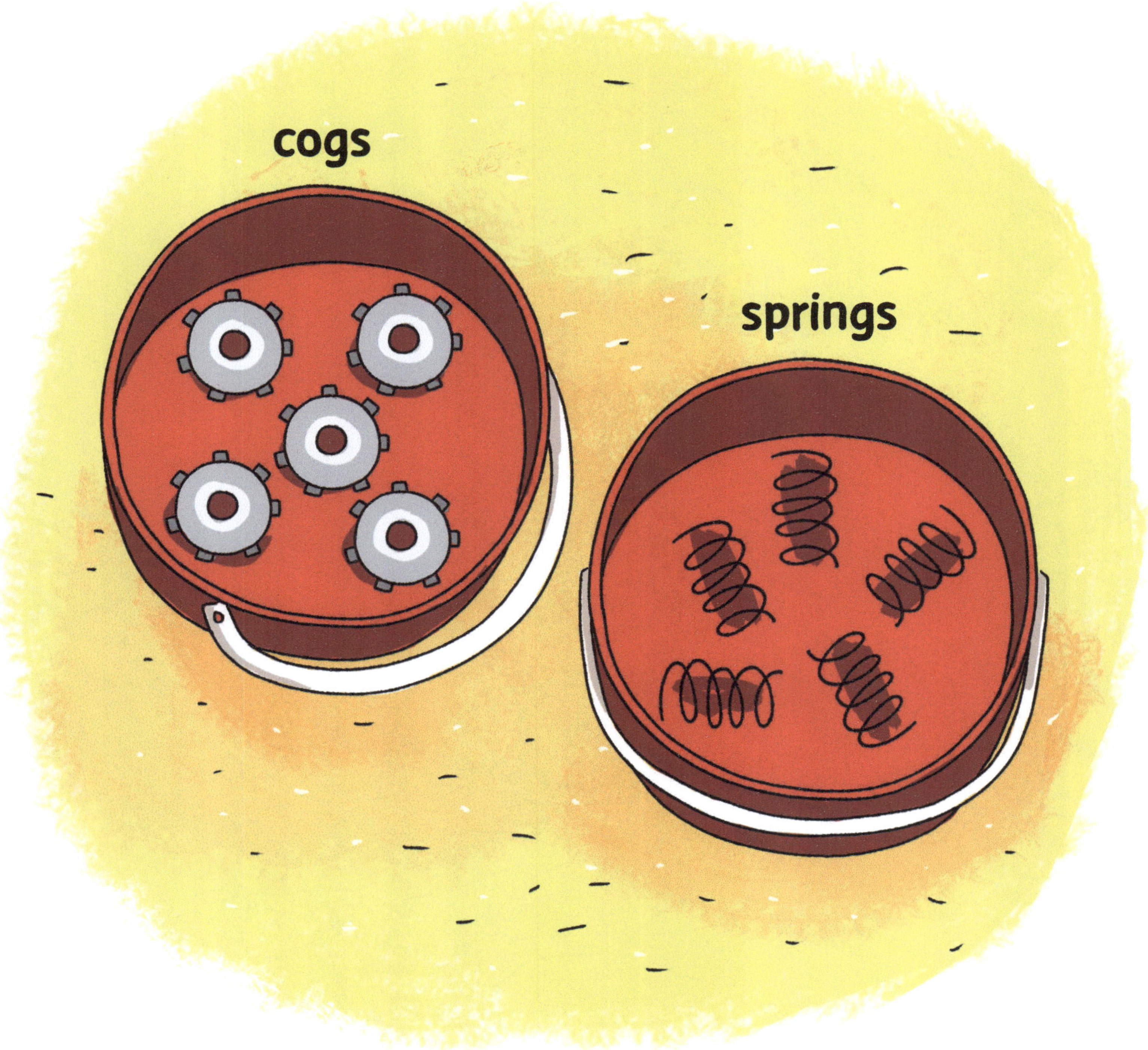

cogs

springs

Look at the cogs and springs. How many cogs are there? How many springs are there? What are the **parts**? What is the **whole**? The **parts** are five and five. The **whole** is ten.

Scooter looked sadly at his broken machine and at the ruined sandcastle towers.

'What shall we do?' he said. 'There isn't enough time left to build lots of new towers.'

‘We might not be able to build the most sandcastle towers, but we can still win the prize for the best decorations,’ said Netty with a smile.

‘Great thinking!’ said Scooter. ‘Let’s make it monster!’

Netty and Scooter began to build new sandcastle towers.

Ralf and Cora collected some shells.

‘How many shells do we have?’ asked Ralf.

Cora counted them. ‘We have seven shells,’ she replied.

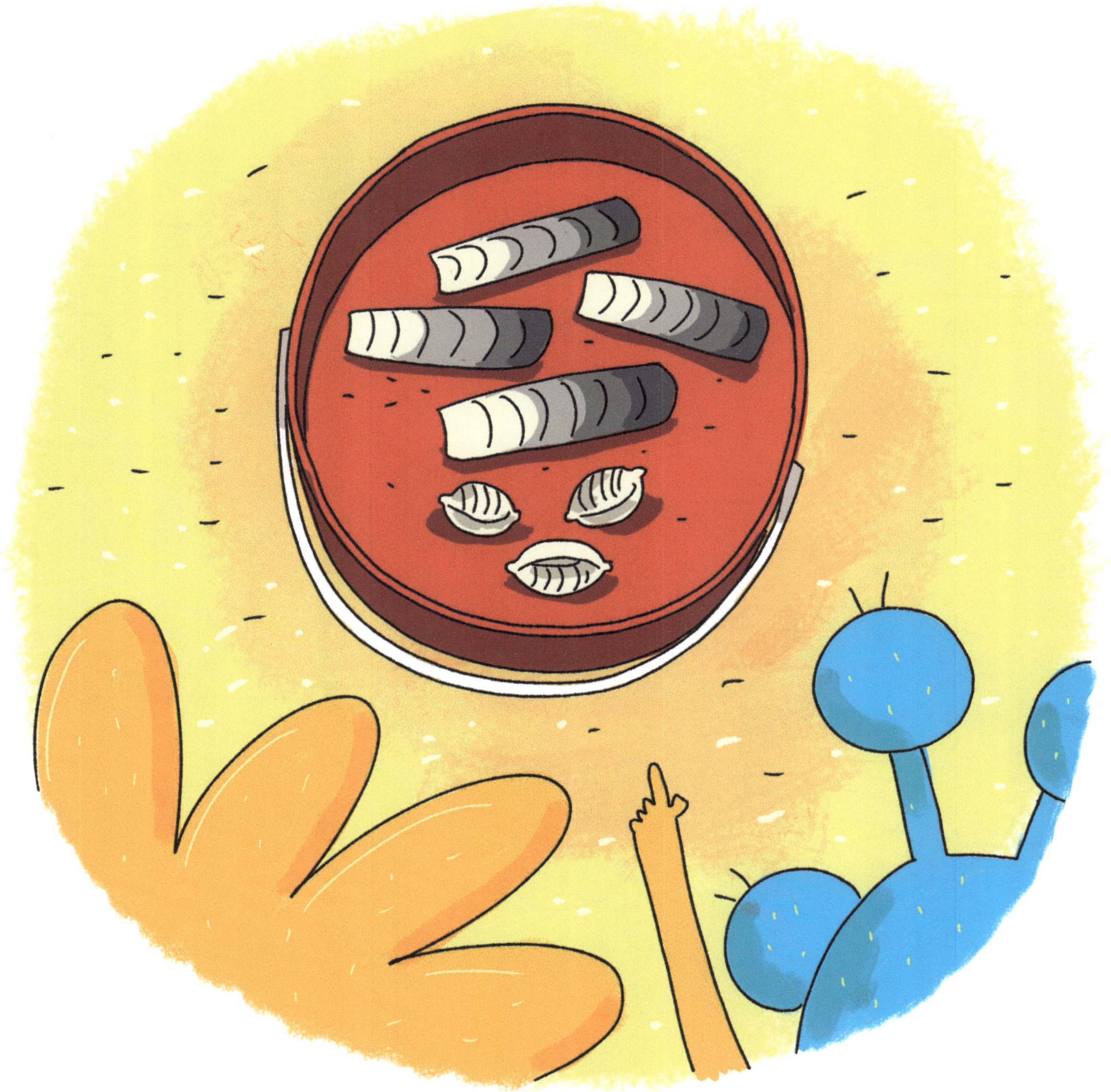

Ralf and Cora’s shells are all together in the bucket. What is the **whole**? The **whole** is seven. There are two types of shell. How many shells of each type are there? What are the **parts**? The **parts** are four and three.

Netty and Scooter looked at the other monsters' sandcastle towers.

'I think the other monsters have got more shells than us,' said Scooter.

Look at the shells. What are the **parts**? What is the **whole**?
The **parts** are four and six. The **whole** is ten.

Scooter was right. The other monsters had collected more shells.

'Why don't we use flags instead?' said Ralf.

‘What else can we use to make our towers look amazing?’ Scooter asked.

‘I think I might have an idea ...’ said Cora.

Later …

'What an imaginative way to decorate your towers! Well done, you have won!' said the judge, giving the monsters a trophy.

The other monsters had won the prize for the most sandcastle towers. Everyone was happy.

The monsters tidied up. Netty put the flags into her bag. Scooter put the cogs and springs into a box, ready to use them to make another machine.

How many cogs and springs are there **altogether**? What is the **whole**? The **whole** is ten. How many cogs are there? How many springs are there? What are the **parts**? The **parts** are five and five.

‘Now, let’s get some ice creams!’ said Ralf.

‘And let’s ask our new friends to come with us,’ said Cora. ‘It will be more fun if we all go together!’

Collecting shells

1. Look at the **part-whole model** below. The **whole** is six. The **parts** are one and five. How many other different ways can you split the **whole** into two **parts**? Use buttons, pasta shapes, or other items to show this. Can zero be a **part**?

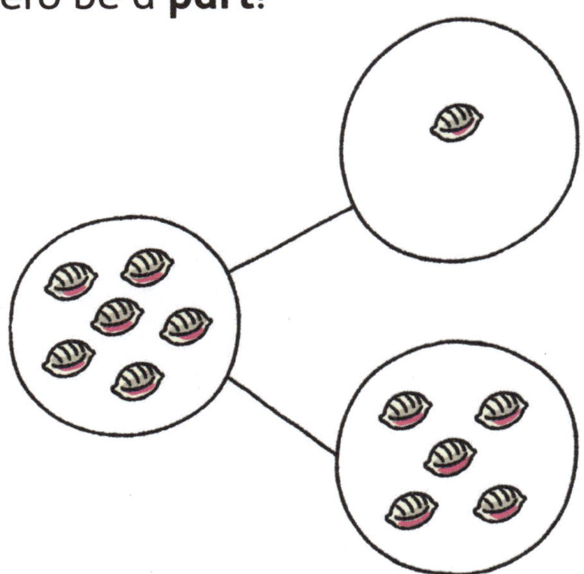

2. How could you put the shells into three **parts** in a different way? Use buttons, pasta shapes, or other items to show this.

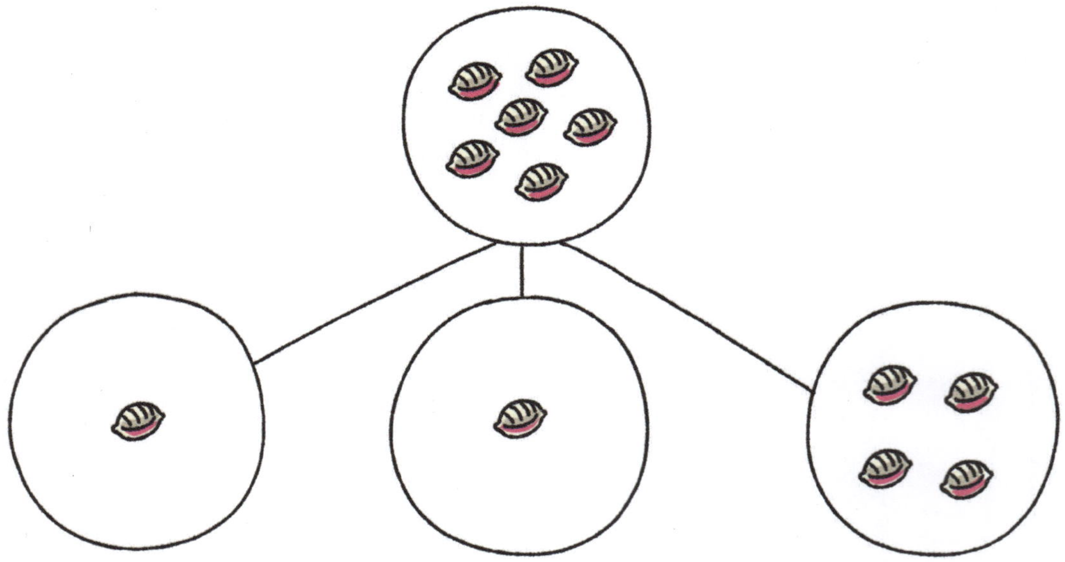

Answers: 1. You can split the **whole** into two **parts** in these ways: zero and six, one and five, two and four, three and three, four and two, five and one, six and zero. Zero can be a **part**. 2. For example, the **parts** could be one, two, and three.